All About Animals

Lions

By Sarah Albee

Reader's Digest Young Families

Contents

Chapter 1

Two Cubs Grow Up

On a hot, windy day, a group of lions sits in the sun-baked grass of a wide-open African plain. But one lion creeps away from the rest. She is looking for a safe place to have her babies.

The mother lion gives birth to two babies. They are tiny, blind, and helpless, completely dependent on their mother. They weigh just about three pounds—less than a bag of flour. It will be three weeks before they start to walk. In the meantime, their mother feeds them and keeps them safe from hungry hyenas and leopards by moving them to different hiding places.

After a few weeks, the mother lion decides it is time for the cubs to meet their father. He and their uncle are the only adult males in the pride.

Wild Words

*A group of lions living together is called a **pride**.*

A few months pass. Early one morning, the cubs kiss their mother good-bye. She and the other females are getting ready to go off to hunt. The cubs' aunt stays behind to watch out for all the little cubs in the pride.

A few hours later, the hunters return. They have not brought back any food. Their hunt was unsuccessful. But they will try again tonight.

Just as she is about to lie down and rest with her cubs, Mother Lion leaps to her feet, growling. She has heard a roar nearby! She knows that male lions from outside her pride may try to take it over. She also knows that her cubs could be in danger if a new male lion becomes the leader. While her cubs hide, she and the other adult females roar fiercely at the stranger. The cubs' father gets ready to do battle. But the stranger changes his mind about attacking. He runs away. The pride is safe!

Do Cubs Hunt?

Cubs start going with their mothers on hunts when they are nearly a year old. They remain dependent on their mothers and other lions for food until they are about two years old.

Cub Care

Lions do not leave their cubs alone and unprotected. If something happens to a mother lion, other females in the pride adopt her cubs.

That evening, the cubs' mother goes hunting again. This time, she and the other hunters manage to kill a large animal. The pride eats well.

After the lions eat, they flop down under a group of trees and take a long nap.

As the years pass, the cubs grow up quickly. The male cub starts to grow a mane. Soon it will be time for him to leave the pride to find his own pride and mate. The female cub will stay in the pride with her mother and other female relatives for the rest of her life.

Chapter 2
The Body of a Lion

Big Cats, Small Cats

If you have a pet cat, you've probably noticed some interesting things about it. It has excellent eyesight and hearing. It moves gracefully—whether it is walking, running, or leaping. It uses its long tail for balance. Your cat often grooms its fur with its tongue. And it sleeps or rests a lot.

Now imagine a cat that does all these things but weighs 500 pounds, is 10 feet long from nose to tail, and has a big mane—a male lion!

Female lions do not have manes and are smaller than the males. They are about 8 feet long and weigh about 300 pounds.

Lions are the only big cat where the male and female look different from each other.

Do lions purr?

Lions can purr, but they don't do it often. Unlike your cat, which can purr while it breathes in and out, lions purr only when they exhale.

Glorious Manes

A male lion's mane starts to grow in at age two or three and is fully grown when the lion is about five years old. The color ranges from pale yellow to black, and the mane gets darker with age.

Some adult male lions have bigger manes than others. A large mane seems to be a status symbol. It gives its owner certain privileges and benefits. For instance, scientists have observed that the lion with the largest mane gets to eat first. And a lion that is getting ready to attack another lion often backs away if the opponent has a large mane.

Fortunately, a mane is mostly fluff and is not heavy. It's a good way to add intimidating size without the accompanying weight.

Manes also protect the lion's head and neck from bites and scratches during fights with other lions.

Baby Teeth

Like human children, lion cubs lose their baby teeth. Their permanent teeth grow in when the cubs are about two years old. Some teeth can be as long as 2 inches, about the length of your pinkie. An adult lion has 30 teeth.

Padded Paws

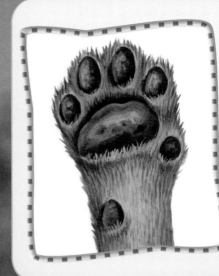

Lions have thick padding on the bottoms of their paws. These special pads help lions move quietly and prevent them from skidding on slippery surfaces, just like your sneakers.

Adult male lions are the only cats with a mane.

Copy Cat

Have you ever watched someone else yawn and then started to yawn yourself? The same thing happens with lions! Yawning, grooming, and roaring all seem to be contagious among lions. If one does it, it sets off a wave across the pride.

Lions can leap an amazing distance in one bound—as far as 35 feet! Their strong muscles also allow them to capture an animal three times their size!

Lions in Action

Lions can run, jump, pounce, climb trees—and even swim if they have to. Like other cats, their backs are flexible. This flexibility, combined with their powerful leg muscles, lets lions leap high in the air and land safely.

Lions also have excellent vision and hearing, like other cats. Lions can see in the dark, and their widely spaced eyes let them see to the sides.

Cool Cats

Lions like to rest during the day, when the sun is hottest. Young lions climb trees to take advantage of cooling breezes. Older, bigger lions look for a shady spot under trees. Sometimes lions lie on their backs to allow the air to cool their undersides.

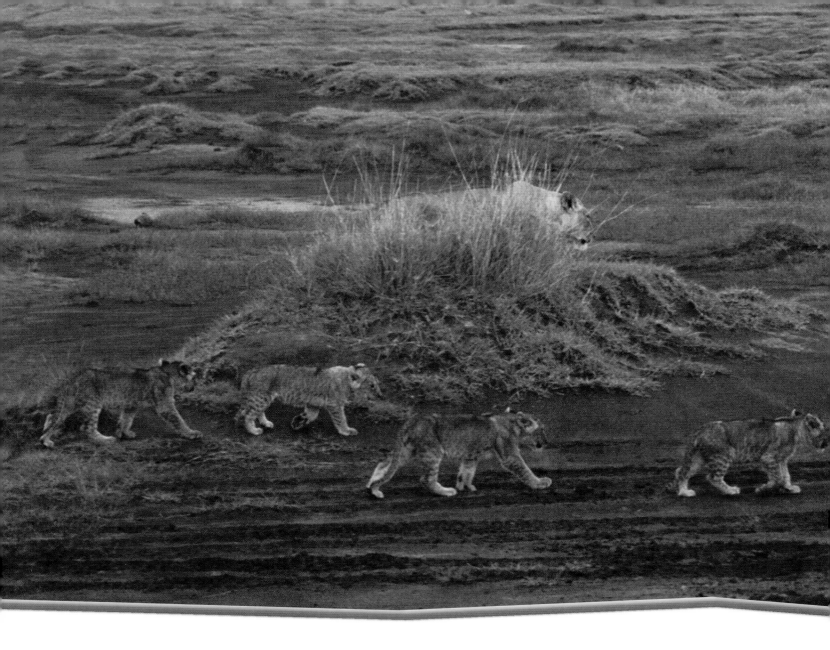

Chapter 3
Lion Families

Lion Cooperation

Lions are the only members of the cat family that work together to raise their young and to hunt for food.

Mothers, daughters, sisters, and female cousins usually live in the same pride their whole lives. Males stay for only a few years.

A Matter of Pride

Why do lions live together in groups? Group living seems to benefit all the lions in the pride. They hunt for food together, groom one another, and take care of one another's babies.

A pride can include as many as 40 lions, but big prides often separate into smaller groups. A pride usually consists of 2 to 18 females and their offspring and 1 to 7 males, with one male as the chief.

If another male challenges the chief lion, there is often a fight for control of the pride. The chief lion tends to be overthrown every three years or so.

The adult females in the group are in charge of caring for the cubs, finding water, deciding where the group will sleep, and hunting for food. If a mother lion dies, other females in the pride adopt her cubs.

When male cubs reach the age of about two or three, they are ready to leave the pride. For a time, they travel without a pride, sometimes in pairs, hunting on their own. Two brothers or male cousins will often remain together for life. When they are fully grown, they try to take control of another pride.

Wild Words

In Africa, the word for lion in Swahili is **simba. Simba** *also means strong and king.*

Heads and Tails

How do lions announce their presence to others? One good way to get attention is to roar! Lions roar to let other lions of their pride know where they are. Males also roar to warn rivals to stay away from their territory. A pride's territory covers about 40 to 50 square miles. This is about the same size as the city of Boston!

Another way lions warn other animals to stay away is by marking their territory. Male lions mark their territory by spraying a combination of urine and scent. The scent is made by special glands at the

base of their tails. Lions put their scent at nose-level, so that other lions can easily detect the odor. They also scratch or claw marks on trees and other places as warnings.

Lions have very expressive faces. They use their facial expressions, as well as their bodies, to communicate. Lions commonly greet one another by head-rubbing and grooming.

Tails Tell the Tale!

Lions are the only members of the cat family with a tuft of fur at the end of their tails. The tuft is useful for communicating with other lions. Lions can see one another's tails above the tall grass and can read the moods of other lions based on tail twitches and back-and-forth movements.

The roar of a lion can sometimes be heard 5 miles away!

Lion cubs love to play. Like human kids, they try to get their parents' attention any way they can!

Playtime

Lion cubs spend a great deal of time playing together. They play-fight, chase one another, and wrestle. Adults occasionally join in the play. A mother lion will flick her tail, allowing the cubs to pounce on it. Much of cubs' play imitates skills they will use as adults, such as stalking and pouncing. Playing together is also an important way for cubs to bond with one another. Often they remain lifelong companions.

Keeping Clean

Lions are careful groomers, keeping their front paws, manes, and chests clean with their rough tongues. Lions groom both themselves and one another. Grooming other lions reinforces social bonds. It also removes more parasites from a lion's fur. A lion grooming itself licks in the same direction the fur grows, but another lion can lick the fur in the opposite direction.

Chapter 4
King of the Beasts

Leaping Lions

Lions are able to sprint as fast as 35 miles per hour—for short distances only. Most of the animals they chase can run a lot faster than that! So lions quietly creep up close to their prey—within 20 or 30 feet—and then dash out and leap onto their victim to try to overpower it.

A lion chasing down prey can run the length of a football field in 6 seconds.

Going on the Hunt

In order to survive, lions spend a lot of their waking time hunting for food. Lions are carnivores, which means they eat other animals. Lions eat gnu, impalas, zebra, gazelles, buffalo, giraffes, wildebeest, antelope, wild boars, and even young hippopotamuses. During hard times, lions eat practically anything—fish, snakes, fruit, and even insects.

Because female lions are smaller and faster than male lions, they are the ones that most often do the hunting for the pride. Lions hunt both in groups and alone.

Over time, lions have learned that they are more successful at catching very large prey when they hunt together. Usually one group of lions circles a potential victim and then stops in front of it. Meanwhile, another group of lions scares the prey from behind, forcing it to run right into the first group of lions.

Young male lions, alone or in pairs, also hunt. Even the chief male in a pride may join a hunt. Sometimes his greater size and strength are needed to bring down an animal much bigger than the females.

Are there any animals that prey on lions?

Lions are at the very top of the food chain, and all other animals tend to avoid them. The only animals that pose a danger to lions are human beings with weapons.

Table Manners

Lion hunts are often unsuccessful. If a group of lion hunters can't catch its prey after a short chase, the lions give up because they are too tired to continue.

Sometimes it's easier to take another animal's food. When lions hear the sound of hyenas, wild dogs, or even other large cats eating, they know where they can get a fast meal! Few animals are foolish enough to protest when hungry lions show up to relieve them of their dinner.

Animals that have died of natural causes are also food for lions. When lions see vultures circling in the air, it is a signal that a carcass is available.

Although females generally bring down prey, it's the males who tend to eat first. Occasionally the females can take a few bites before the males chase them away. When the male lions are finished eating, the females get their turn. Only then are the cubs and young lions allowed to eat. Some of the more aggressive cubs sneak in and eat with the males while the rest of the pride keeps a respectful distance.

An adult male lion can eat as much as 90 pounds of meat in just one meal.

Lions do a lot of resting and sleeping—as much as 20 hours in a 24-hour day!

Big-Cat Naps

Lions do most of their hunting at night or very early in the morning, when the air is cooler. When they find food, lions gorge themselves, eating as much as they can and then some more! They know from experience that it might be several days before they have another successful hunt and are able to eat again.

Lions often like to take a nap after eating a large meal. Resting is a good way for lions to conserve energy. Hunting is hard work!

Other animals often graze close to resting or sleeping lions and don't seem at all frightened or concerned. They appear to understand that lions resting out in the open pose no danger to them.

Always Room for Seconds!

Lions have expandable stomachs that stretch, allowing lions to eat huge amounts of food at one time. They may then go three or four days without eating again.

Chapter 5
Lions in the World

Lion Habitat

Although most lions live on savannas, some live in wooded areas with open spaces. Lions are able to survive in extreme drought conditions, including deserts.

Wild Words

A **savanna** is a hot grassland area with scattered trees. It has two seasons—a long dry one and a short one with very heavy rains. During the dry season, the grass dries out and turns golden-brown.

Lions are the light-brown color of sun-dried grass. Their color helps them blend into their surroundings and sneak up on their prey.

Lands of the Lions
Past and Present

☐ The **green** area shows where lions lived in the past.
■ The **blue** areas show where they live today.

Thousands of years ago, lions lived in Europe, Asia, and even on our own continent of North America. But due to changes in climate, hunting by humans, and the growth of farms and cities, the habitat of lions has decreased enormously. So has the number of lions. Today almost all the lions on Earth live in Africa. Scientists are not sure exactly how many lions live in Africa, but some estimate that there are fewer than 50,000. A few hundred live in India.

The Future of Lions

In order to survive, lions need enough land to roam on and plenty of animals to catch and eat. As humans have continued to build farms, houses, and factories on more and more wild lands, the areas where lions can wander freely have grown smaller and smaller.

Most of the lions in Africa and all of the lions in India live in national parks and preserves that are protected. But now even this land, which is set aside for lions and other wildlife, is being threatened by population growth and the expanded need for more farmland. To protect lions from disappearing completely, it is important to protect the land that has been set aside for them.

You Can Help!

Become a member of a conservation group that works to protect the habitats of lions. It may even be your local zoo.

Fast Facts About Lions

Scientific name	*Panthera leo*
Class	Mammals
Order	Carnivora
Size	Males about 8 feet in length, not including tail
	Females about 5 feet in length, not including tail
Weight	Males to 500 pounds
	Females to 300 pounds
Life span	About 15 years in the wild
	About 30 years in captivity
Habitat	Savannas and open wooded areas
Top speed	35 miles per hour in short bursts

Cat Spots!

Lions are born with spotted coats! The spots fade as the lions grow up.

Glossary of Wild Words

carcass   the body of a dead animal

carnivore   a meat-eating animal

conservation   the protection and preservation of land, animals, plants, and other natural resources

cub   a young meat-eating **mammal**

drought   a long period of time without rain

ecosystem   all the living and nonliving things in a certain environment

genus   a large category of related plants or animals consisting of smaller groups (**species**) of closely related plants or animals

grooming   cleaning of fur, skin, or feathers by an animal

habitat   the natural environment where an animal or a plant lives

hyena   a meat-eating mammal that resembles a dog, found in Africa and Asia

mammal	an animal with a backbone and hair on its body that drinks milk from its mother when it is born	**pride**	a group of lions that live together
mane	long hair on the head or neck of an animal	**savanna**	a flat grassland area with scattered trees in a hot region of the world
plain	a large, flat area of land, usually without trees	**simba**	the Swahili word for lion, strong, and king
predator	an animal that hunts and eats other animals to survive	**species**	a group of plants or animals that are the same in many ways
preserves	areas of land or water where plants and animals are protected	**territory**	an area of land that an animal considers to be its own and will fight to defend
prey	animals that are hunted by other animals for food	**victim**	a living thing that is hunted or killed

Index